CARING FOR MACAQUE MONKEY

PET OWNERS GUIDE

THE PLEASURES AND DIFFICULTIES OF OWNING MACAQUES AS PETS

DR REIS FERNANDEZ

Copyright© 2024 **DR REIS FERNANDEZ**

All rights reserved. No part or part of this book or publication may be reproduced, stored, or transferred in any form by electronic, mechanical, recording, or other retrieval system without written permission from the publisher

Table of Contents

INTRODUCTION 5

CHAPTER 1 7

RECOGNIZING THE NEEDS AND BEHAVIOR OF MACAQUES 7

CHAPTER 2 12

SELECTING THE APPROPRIATE MACAQUE BREED FOR YOUR WAY OF LIFE 12

CHAPTER 3 17

LEGAL AND ETHICAL ASPECTS OF MACAQUE OWNERSHIP 17

CHAPTER 4 23

MACAQUE HOUSING AND ENCLOSURE DESIGN 23

CHAPTER 5 29

VETERINARIAN AND HEALTH CONCERNS FOR MACAQUES 29

CHAPTER 6 36

MACAQUE ENRICHMENT AND MENTAL STIMULATION 36

CHAPTER 7 ....**43**

METHODS OF SOCIALIZATION AND TRAINING FOR MACAQUES ...43

CHAPTER 8 ....**51**

MACAQUE HANDLING AND SAFETY PROCEDURES 51

CHAPTER 9 ....**59**

TYPICAL PROBLEMS AND FIXES FOR MACAQUE CARE 59

CHAPTER 10 ....**70**

HAVING A HAPPY AND MEANINGFUL BOND WITH YOUR MACAQUE PET..70

CHAPTER 11 ....**80**

FREQUENTLY ASKED QUESTIONS (FAQS) CONCERNING OWNING PET MACAQUES 80

Introduction

Macaques are bright, gregarious monkeys renowned for their varied behaviours and cognitive ability. While some individuals may be drawn to the thought of having a macaque companion, it's critical to understand the difficulties of their care and well-being. Keeping a macaque as a pet may be an exciting and gratifying experience, but it also presents new problems and obligations.

This book attempts to give helpful insights and recommendations to ensure the well-being of both you and your pet. Whether you're thinking about bringing a macaque into your home or are already a proud macaque owner looking for advice, we'll go over the practical aspects of their care, the ethical considerations surrounding their ownership, and the joys and challenges of living with one of these remarkable creatures.

This guide will cover a variety of topics, including how to understand macaque behaviour and needs, ethical and legal issues, selecting the best species for your lifestyle, designing appropriate housing and enclosures, adhering to dietary recommendations, health care considerations, enrichment tactics, training methods, safety procedures, and common problems encountered by macaque owners.

Let's embark on this journey together and enjoy the delights of living with a macaque pet. With information and understanding, you may embark on a joyful journey with your macaque partner, cultivating a friendship based on trust, respect, and companionship while promoting the welfare and happiness of these remarkable creatures.

Chapter 1

Recognizing the Needs and Behavior of Macaques

Macaques, members of the Cercopithecidae family, are highly intelligent and sociable primates with a diverse variety of behaviours and complicated demands. In this in-depth investigation of macaque behaviour and requirements, we will look at natural behaviours, social structures, communication tactics, environmental demands, and the implications for domestic macaque care.

Understanding macaque natural behaviours is crucial for giving effective care in captivity. Macaques are found in Asia, Africa, and Gibraltar. To adapt to their natural settings, animals have evolved a wide range of behaviours like as hunting for food, grooming, socialising, mating, and territorial defence.

In social organisations, social contacts promote group cohesiveness and communication. Macaques live in complex social groupings characterised by hierarchical hierarchies. Individuals in a group form dominance hierarchies through a range of interactions, including as violence, submission, and alliances. Dominance determines access to resources like as food, mates, and favoured resting areas.

Macaques communicate by facial expressions, bodily postures, and movements such as grooming, play-fighting, and presenting. They also utilise vocalisations for group communication. Vocalisations can range from warning cries to friendly vocalisations, with each having a distinct communication function.

Macaques are flexible and may survive in a variety of circumstances, provided their fundamental needs are satisfied. In their native habitats, macaques live in a variety of environments, including forests, grasslands, and cities. Enrichment activities, such as puzzle feeders, climbing structures, and sensory stimulation, are critical for fostering mental and physical health in both captive and wild macaques.

Nutritional Requirements: Provide a balanced food to suit the nutritional demands of captive animals. Fresh fruits and vegetables should make up the majority of their food, supplemented with high-quality primate pellets and occasional treats. Macaques are omnivorous and eat a variety of fruits, vegetables, leaves, seeds, insects, and small animals. It's also critical to avoid feeding kids hazardous or unhealthy meals.

Many macaque species reproduce seasonally, with females displaying genital swellings to signal fertility. Gestation times vary by species, ranging from several months to more than a year. Infants are cared for by their mothers and the greater social group, and they learn essential skills via observation and interaction. Macaque social dynamics are heavily influenced by reproduction, with dominant individuals often having priority access to mates.

Macaques possess high cognitive abilities such as problem-solving, tool usage, and social learning, allowing them to absorb complicated concepts and adapt to changing surroundings. Puzzle toys and training sessions are examples of stimulating activities that keep captives' minds engaged and prevent boredom.

Understanding macaques' natural preferences and needs is critical for providing appropriate care and ensuring their well-being in the home setting. We can improve the quality of life for macaques in captivity by creating exciting environments, fostering social involvement, and responding to their nutritional and mental needs.

Chapter 2

Selecting the Appropriate Macaque Breed for Your Way of Life

When selecting a companion animal, you must examine a number of things, including your lifestyle, living circumstances, experience level, and each species' specific requirements and qualities. In this comprehensive guide, we will look at the numerous macaque species that may be kept as pets, as well as their unique characteristics, care requirements, and compatibility for different families.

The genus Macaca has around 23 species, including the rhesus macaque (Macaca mulatta), Japanese macaque (Macaca fuscata), and pig-tailed macaque (Macaca nemestrina). Each of these species has distinct traits, ranging from size and appearance to behaviour and environmental preferences. It is critical to conduct considerable study on each species to determine which one best suits your needs and lifestyle.

When picking a macaque species, consider space needs and handling capabilities at different sizes. For example, the Japanese macaque is distinguished by its unusual red face and strong body, whilst the pig-tailed macaque has a distinguishing tuft of hair at the end of its tail. Macaque species vary greatly in size.

When selecting a macaque species, consider your ability to manage and communicate with diverse temperaments. Macaque temperaments and behavioural inclinations vary according on social organisation, natural environment, and individual upbringing. Some species, such as the rhesus macaque, are noted for their forceful and occasionally violent behaviour, but others, such as the Japanese macaque, may be more docile and adaptive.

Macaques are extremely sociable creatures who thrive in the company of their conspecifics, despite varying social dynamics between species (e.g., tight dominance hierarchies or more egalitarian societies). As a result, you should consider if you have the time, money, and knowledge to support a macaque's social demands, including providing chances for socialisation and enrichment.

Macaque species have diverse food preferences, including fruits, vegetables, insects, and small animals. It is essential to understand the dietary requirements of the species you have chosen in order to give a nutritious diet and avoid health complications. You should also consider each species' specific care demands, which may include veterinarian treatment, habitat enrichment, and grooming requirements.

Research the legal and ethical implications of owning a macaque before adopting one as a pet. Some nations have highly severe rules governing primates' ownership, requiring permits, inspections, and adherence to welfare standards. You should also consider the moral implications of keeping a wild animal in captivity, and ensure that you can provide your macaque partner with an appropriate and rewarding habitat.

Choosing the right macaque breed for your lifestyle depends on things including living arrangements, availability, experience, and dedication to giving proper care. You should also consider if you have the time, space, money, and dedication to provide long-term care for a macaque, as well as your ability to cope with any obstacles like as behavioural issues, veterinary needs, and socialisation requirements.

By carefully analysing the qualities, requirements, and compatibility of various macaque species, you may find the appropriate companion animal to enrich your life and provide a caring and rewarding home for a monkey friend. Do your study, talk with experienced specialists, and make your decision based on the requirements of both you and your possible macaque partner.

Chapter 3

Legal and Ethical Aspects of Macaque Ownership

Because macaques have complex social, behavioural, and welfare demands, keeping them as pets raises a variety of legal and ethical concerns. In this in-depth research, we will look at the legal structure governing macaque ownership, ethical concerns about their wellbeing in captivity, and the ramifications for persons who are considering or are already keeping macaques as companions.

Macaque ownership laws may include permits, licences, or registrations for possession, breeding, sale, and transit. The legality of keeping macaques as pets varies widely among jurisdictions, and is governed by national, state/provincial, and municipal authorities. Many nations have strict regulations or outright bans on the ownership of primates, especially macaques, owing to concerns about public safety, animal welfare, and conservation.

Legal measures to preserve the welfare of macaques may exist in regions where their ownership is legal. These policies often contain minimum standards for housing, care, and treatment, as well as facilities for veterinary care, enrichment, and socialisation. Owners who breach animal welfare rules may face fines, penalties, seizure of their animals, and legal consequences.

Macaques are protected under international and national conservation regimes due to their wild status and environmental importance. Keeping macaques as pets can jeopardise conservation efforts by encouraging illicit wildlife trafficking, habitat damage, and disturbance of natural populations. To mitigate these dangers, responsible ownership methods such as lawful acquisition, proper documentation, and ethical handling are essential.

Keeping macaques as pets presents ethical concerns regarding psychological health, animal welfare, species conservation, and human-animal interactions. Macaques are extremely clever, gregarious creatures with complex physical, emotional, and behavioural requirements that can be difficult to fulfil in captivity. Other ethical concerns include the risk of stress, social isolation, loss of natural behaviours, and bodily and psychological damage.

Ethical ownership of macaques includes providing adequate habitat, enrichment, socialisation, and veterinary treatment to suit their complex demands. Macaques housed in tiny cages, isolated from other macaques, and with few chances for mental and physical stimulation can become bored, frustrated, and exhibit stereotyped behaviours. Inadequate housing, social impoverishment, dietary deficits, and a lack of veterinary treatment can all contribute to a variety of welfare difficulties.

Macaques may be dangerous to humans due to their innate impulses and behaviours. Bite injuries, zoonotic infections, and property damage are all possible concerns linked with macaque ownership. Responsible ownership procedures, such as safe handling, training, and containment, are critical for reducing these dangers. Because of their strength, agility, and aggressive potential, keeping macaques as pets endangers human health and safety.

Alternatives to Macaque Ownership: Given ethical and legal concerns around macaque ownership, individuals may consider alternative methods to connect with these animals. Opportunities to view macaques in reputable zoological institutions, participate in animal conservation programmes, and support research and educational initiatives can all lead to meaningful contact with macaques while helping to advance their conservation and wellbeing.

Responsible ownership of macaques as pets is essential for ensuring their care and compliance with legal and ethical criteria. These practices include obtaining macaques from reputable suppliers, providing suitable housing and enrichment, following welfare laws and regulations, and encouraging responsible management of these beautiful creatures.

To summarise, ethical ownership practices, educated decision-making, and a dedication to macaque welfare and conservation are critical for fostering beneficial results for both the animals and humans involved in their captive care. The legal and ethical issues surrounding the keeping of macaques as pets are complicated and varied, necessitating careful analysis and respect to laws, regulations, and moral values.

Chapter 4

Macaque Housing and Enclosure Design

Meeting the physiological, behavioural, and psychological demands of captive macaques necessitates the development of appropriate housing and enclosure designs. In this extensive research, we will look at the most significant aspects of creating macaque habitats, such as enclosure size and architecture, environmental enrichment, safety elements, and maintenance processes.

Macaques are extremely gregarious, arboreal primates that require ample room for climbing, exploration, social engagement, and cerebral stimulation. They flourish in conditions that are similar to their native habitats, allowing for physical exercise, social bonding, and foraging behaviour. As a result, it is critical to understand macaques' natural behaviours and needs before creating enclosures for them.

Enclosures for macaques should be big, with numerous levels, platforms, and climbing equipment to promote natural behaviours such as climbing, swinging, and leaping. A wide range of surfaces, including grass, sand, and branches, can provide sensory stimulation and enrichment. The size and shape of the enclosures should meet the occupants' demands while also offering ample area for mobility, enrichment, and social contact.

To enhance the environment, enrichment activities should mirror natural behaviours, encourage problem-solving, and provide opportunity for exploration and socialisation. Enrichment items include puzzle feeders, foraging possibilities, climbing structures, ropes, swings, and unusual things. Rotating enrichment on a regular basis can help reduce habituation and boredom.

Environmental enrichment is critical for macaques' physical and psychological well-being while in confinement.

Adding natural elements like plants, trees, rocks, logs, and water can enhance the sensory experience and mimic the complexity of macaque environments. Natural surfaces, such as sand or dirt, can help macaques perform digging, foraging, and scent-marking behaviours. Providing opportunities for sun exposure and fresh air also benefits macaques' overall health.

To ensure safety, macaque cages should be made of durable materials that can withstand gnawing, burrowing, and climbing. To keep macaques from entering or exiting harmful places, mesh or wire obstacles must be securely fixed. Locking mechanisms and escape-proof doors are essential for both normal maintenance and emergency scenarios. Enclosures must be safe and secure to prevent escapes, injuries, and interactions with people or other animals.

To ensure macaques' health and comfort, enclosures should be kept at the appropriate temperature and environment. Provide access to both sunny and shady places so that macaques may adjust their body temperature accordingly. Heating and cooling systems may be necessary to keep the enclosure at the desired temperature all year, especially in places with harsh weather or seasonal variations.

To prevent disease transmission and maintain hygienic standards, enclosures for macaques should be easy to clean, disinfect, and handle waste. Accessible holding spaces, chutes, and transfer tunnels can allow macaques move safely during medical operations or exams.

When building cages for macaques, consider their social dynamics. Enclosures should reduce competition for resources like as food, water, and resting spots; they should facilitate the creation of social hierarchies, give chances for social bonding and grooming, and resolve conflicts between individuals or subgroups within larger populations.

Maintenance protocols ensure the health, hygiene, and lifespan of macaque cages. Protocols that should be followed include daily spot cleaning, the elimination of garbage and uneaten food, and occasional deep cleaning and disinfection. Enclosure structures, equipment, and enrichment items should all be evaluated regularly for signs of wear, damage, or deterioration and fixed or replaced as needed.

Designing enclosures for macaques requires adherence to relevant legislation, standards, and recommendations for captive primate care. These rules might include national, international, or municipal legislation governing enclosure size, building materials, safety features, environmental enrichment, veterinary care, and animal welfare.

To summarise, creating housing and enclosure conditions that are appropriate for macaques requires considering their behavioural, physiological, and social needs, as well as complying to legal and ethical standards. By creating exciting, safe, and rewarding habitats, we may improve the health, well-being, and natural behaviours of macaques in captivity while also fostering meaningful relationships with these incredible primates.

Chapter 5

Veterinarian and Health Concerns for Macaques

In this comprehensive research, we will look at the most important aspects of health care and veterinary concerns for macaques, such as preventative care, medical management, nutrition, husbandry methods, and emergency procedures. Providing adequate health care to macaques is critical for their survival and well-being while in captivity.

Preventive treatment is crucial for maintaining the health and vigour of captive macaques. Routine veterinarian checks, immunisations, and parasite control techniques help to avoid disease and detect it early. When creating preventive care regimens for macaques, it is important to account their age, gender, reproductive status, and medical history.

Veterinarians check macaques' health using physical examinations, blood testing, faecal analysis, dental evaluations, and imaging investigations. Veterinary appointments can provide an opportunity to discuss preventative care, nutrition, behaviour, and husbandry techniques with carers. Regular veterinarian inspections provide complete health assessments, monitoring of vital signs, and early diagnosis of potential health issues.

Immunisations are essential for protecting macaques from infectious illnesses while in captivity. Hepatitis, polio, measles, and tetanus are among the most common immunisations for macaques. Vaccination methods should be designed collaboratively with veterinarians and tailored to the macaque population's specific risk factors and epidemiological concerns.

To protect macaques from parasites, frequent deworming, flea and tick prevention, and ectoparasite control procedures are recommended. Carers should keep a look out for indicators of parasite infections in macaques, including as itching, hair loss, gastrointestinal disorders, and lethargy, and contact veterinarians for the best treatment options.

Macaques require a well-balanced diet consisting of fruits, vegetables, leafy greens, nuts, seeds, cereals, and high-quality monkey pellets. Caretakers should collaborate with veterinarians and nutritionists to create food regimens that support good health while avoiding nutritional deficits or imbalances. Macaques' health and lifespan are heavily reliant on their food requirements, which vary according to species, age, gender, reproductive state, and activity level.

Proper husbandry procedures meet the physical, social, and behavioural demands of macaques while minimising stress and welfare problems. Carers should adhere to established husbandry practices, maintain clean and hygienic living circumstances, provide chances for social contact and mental stimulation, and keep a constant eye on macaques for symptoms of disease or suffering. Husbandry methods encompass a wide range of everyday care and management activities.

Carers should regularly monitor behavioural indicators of health, including activity level, appetite, social interactions, grooming behaviour, posture, vocalisations, and general demeanour, to identify potential health issues. Any variations from normal behaviour should be addressed immediately and reported to veterinary specialists for further examination and treatment.

In case of an emergency, carers should have mechanisms in place to notify veterinary specialists, administer first aid, secure the surroundings, and move macaques to veterinary facilities. Emergency kits should be immediately available and well equipped with supplies, drugs, and medical equipment to handle common situations such trauma, respiratory distress, and allergic reactions. Emergency readiness is critical for efficiently reacting to medical emergencies, injuries, or abrupt health problems affecting macaques.

To prevent zoonotic disease transmission in captive macaques, practise regular handwashing, surface disinfection, and proper handling of potentially infected objects. Macaques can spread illnesses to humans by direct contact, consuming contaminated food or water, or being exposed to infected bodily fluids. To prevent zoonotic disease transmission, carers should practise excellent hygiene, use personal protective equipment while handling macaques or their excrement, and follow correct sanitation practices.

Working with Veterinary Experts:

The health and well-being of macaques in captivity are significantly reliant on teamwork between carers and veterinarians. The latter are essential for developing and implementing health care protocols, diagnosing and treating medical disorders, providing preventative care, and providing advise on diet, husbandry practices, and emergency preparedness. Carers should work cooperatively with veterinary practitioners to gain information and help in maintaining macaque health and wellbeing.

In conclusion, providing proper health care and veterinary considerations for macaques in captivity requires a comprehensive approach that includes preventive care, medical management, nutrition, husbandry practices, behavioural monitoring, emergency procedures, and collaboration with veterinary professionals. Carers can maintain the long-term health, happiness, and vigour of these wonderful monkeys by prioritising macaque welfare and using evidence-based healthcare regimens.

Chapter 6

Macaque Enrichment and Mental Stimulation

To ensure the best possible care for macaques in captivity, enrichment and mental stimulation are required. These activities mimic natural behaviours, promote mental and physical health, keep captive macaques engaged, and increase their overall quality of life. In this extensive study, we will look at a number of enrichment strategies, environmental changes, and cognitive tests designed to spark macaques' attention and suit their complex behavioural needs.

Recognise the value of enrichment.
The phrase "enrichment" refers to activities and stimulation that benefit caged animals' mental, physical, and emotional wellbeing. Enrichment is critical for preventing boredom, decreasing stress, developing

natural behaviours, and engaging the intellect in macaques. To suit macaques' specific requirements and preferences, enrichment activities must be diverse, species-appropriate, and customised.

Environmental enrichment involves modifying the physical surrounds of macaque cages to increase sensory experiences and promote natural behaviours. Examples include climbing, swinging, leaping, foraging, grooming, socialising, and exploring. Naturalistic substrates, plants, climbing frames, ropes, perches, platforms, hiding areas, and water features are all effective ways to improve the habitat.

Enhancing sociable Relations: Macaques thrive in the companionship of their conspecifics, making them very sociable creatures. Participating in social enrichment activities encourages group members to communicate, collaborate, and establish stronger social relationships.

Examples include grooming, play, wrestling, chasing, vocalising, and food sharing. To sustain intrinsic social dynamics, social enrichment might include building stable social groupings or introducing complementary individuals.

Cognitive enrichment exercises encourage macaques to improve their memory, problem-solving, and decision-making abilities. Examples include puzzle feeders, food-dispensing toys, manipulables, nesting materials, smell trails, and new stimuli. The complexity and difficulty of cognitive enrichment activities can vary, allowing macaques to experiment, try new things, and change their behaviour to get the desired effects.

Sensory enrichment allows macaques to enhance their senses, including sight, hearing, smell, touch, and taste. This might include adjusting them to new tastes, textures, noises, scents, and visual stimuli. Sensory enrichment can improve the overall sensory experience of captive macaques by encouraging curiosity, exploration, and sensory discrimination.

Rotating enrichment devices, features, and buildings help keep macaques' enclosures fresh and prevent habituation over time. It is advised that carers vary the sorts of enrichment provided to macaques, reorganise existing structures, and introduce new objects on a regular basis. Environmental rotation keeps macaques busy and engaged by introducing different barriers and stimuli.

Training and behavioural conditioning can improve interactions between macaques and their carers. When educated using positive reinforcement strategies, macaques may learn new behaviours, engage in cooperative care routines, and select to participate in enrichment activities. Training sessions can increase communication, strengthen human-animal bonds, and offer macaques more autonomy and decision-making abilities.

Food-based enrichment involves engaging macaques in activities related to food and their natural foraging tendencies. This might include dispersing food across the enclosure, concealing food in puzzle feeders, presenting food in novel ways, and offering a variety of flavours and textures. Food-based enrichment encourages macaques to employ their senses, dexterity, and problem-solving skills to seek and eat food.

Macaques can use tools and manipulate objects to complete tasks and collect resources effectively. Enrichment activities including manipulating and utilising tools can help to stimulate macaques' natural behaviours and cognitive abilities. This might include providing items that must be constructed or handled, such as puzzle toys, manipulable objects, and devices that, when used correctly, provide rewards.

Unique and diverse cages for macaques promote interest, exploration, and adaptability. Carers may provide macaques with dynamic and fascinating settings by introducing new items, textures, scents, noises, and social companions. In addition to minimising habituation and keeping macaques intellectually engaged, novelty and diversity encourage them to explore and interact with their surroundings.

To ensure the safety of macaques during enrichment activities, carers must prioritise safety measures. It is critical that enrichment products be composed of durable, non-toxic materials that can withstand manipulation, chewing, and biting. To ensure macaques' safety, carers should inspect enrichment objects on a regular basis for signs of wear, breakage, or possible risks. If required, they should be removed or replaced.

To summarise, enrichment and mental stimulation are critical components of providing the best possible care for captive macaques. Carers may enhance captive macaques' physical, cognitive, and emotional well-being while addressing their natural needs and behaviours through a range of exciting enrichment activities. To ensure the overall well-being and happiness of macaques in captivity, enrichment activities should be tailored to their specific preferences and talents and supplied on a regular basis.

Chapter 7

Methods of Socialization and Training for Macaques

Providing the best possible care for macaques in captivity involves both socialisation and training. These techniques establish social links within macaque groups, promote cooperative behaviour, enhance cognitive stimulation, and foster good relationships with carers. In this comprehensive research, we will look at a number of training and socialisation tactics tailored to macaques' unique needs and abilities.

Positive reinforcement approaches are used in teaching macaques to foster desirable behaviours and cooperative relationships with carers. When a goal behaviour is accomplished, positive reinforcement involves supplying macaques with desired stimuli—such as food, toys, or social interactions—as quickly as feasible. Patience, consistency, and clear communication are three critical components of every effective training programme.

Target training is the process of teaching macaques to touch or follow a specific object, such as a stick, ball, or hand-held target. This strategy allows carers to urge macaques to migrate to certain regions of their cage, direct their movements, and position them for veterinary treatments. Additionally, target training can aid in the acquisition of progressively harder activities and behaviours.

Positive reinforcement enhances the likelihood of repeating a behaviour by offering favourable cues to macaques after exhibiting it. Rewards might take the shape of food, verbal praise, physical reinforcement, access to favourite hobbies, and social connections.

Reward distribution must be prompt and consistent in order to reinforce desired behaviours and foster a favourable link with training.

Desensitisation and counterconditioning are techniques used to reduce fear or aversion to certain stimuli or situations. This includes gradually and subtly introducing the feared or unpleasant stimuli to macaques, while rewarding tranquil, complacent behaviour. Macaques eventually lose their dread and anxiety as they learn to correlate the previously feared stimuli with pleasant experiences.

Chaining and shaping include breaking down complex behaviours into smaller, more manageable steps and rewarding progress towards the desired outcome. This strategy allows macaques to progressively learn new abilities and behaviours while keeping their present ones. Chaining occurs when many behaviours are connected together in a sequential order, with one acting as a cue or reinforcement for the one that comes after it.

Socialisation involves building favourable ties between macaques and their carers. Socialisation tactics include cooperative feeding activities, supervised play sessions, grooming exchanges, and introductions to pairs or groups. Socialisation promotes collaboration, communication, and social bonding among macaques and increases their overall well-being.

Establishing pleasant relationships, routines, and progressive introductions with caretakers is crucial when introducing apes to them for the first time. Carers may build trust and rapport with macaques by spending time near their cage, chatting gently, distributing treats, and acting in a non-threatening manner. Macaques become less irritated and more cooperative during handling and care operations as they learn to recognise and respond positively to their carers.

Cooperative care training involves teaching macaques to participate in their own medical procedures, including veterinarian exams, blood draws, and medicine delivery. Macaques learn to cooperate with carers during routine health examinations, present body parts, and remain still through the use of positive reinforcement strategies. Training in cooperative care reduces stress and anxiety, eliminates the need for medication or restraint, and enhances the macaques' overall well-being.

Macaques learn skills by observing and imitating their peers. This is known as social education. Allowing macaques to see and interact with humans, even older, more experienced group members, is an important aspect of social learning strategies. Macaques learn new behaviours, skills, and information through social learning, which allows them to succeed in their adaptive roles and integrate into the community.

Training can address undesirable behaviours, enrichment activities, and specific behavioural issues in macaques. Macaques can be educated to participate in enrichment activities such as puzzle feeders, foraging exercises, or interactive toys to stimulate their minds and keep them entertained. Positive reinforcement approaches may also be used in training to redirect or change unwanted behaviours such as excessive vocalisations, violent behaviour, or stereotyped behaviour.

Effective training and socialisation for macaques require consistency and repetition. Frequent training sessions with clear information, reliable methods, and consistent reinforcement of desirable behaviours are required. Repetition builds confidence and trust between macaques and their carers, as well as consistent behaviour and learning reinforcement.

Customise exercise programmes for macaques based on their specific needs, interests, and skill levels. Training strategies should be tailored to each macaque's unique qualities, personality attributes, and learning style. To achieve beneficial results, carers should monitor and analyse each macaque's behaviour, identify areas for development or enrichment, and adjust training techniques as needed.

In conclusion, training and socialisation tactics are critical for improving the mental, emotional, and physical health of macaques confined in captivity. Carers may encourage good interactions, facilitate adaptive behaviours, and improve the overall well-being of macaques in captivity by using cooperative care training, desensitisation, socialisation, and positive reinforcement techniques. It is critical to offer a quiet and fulfilling environment for these remarkable primates by teaching and socialising them with patience, consistency, and respect for their individual needs and skills.

Chapter 8

Macaque handling and safety procedures

The safety and well-being of macaques in captivity necessitates cautious handling and adherence to established guidelines. Macaques are powerful, clever, and agile creatures, therefore managing them necessitates careful consideration of their unique characteristics, behaviour, and temperament. Through an in-depth research, we will look at the core principles, strategies, and safety considerations for managing macaques in various situations.

To effectively handle macaques, carers must understand their behaviour, social structure, and communication signs. Age, sex, reproductive status, and temperamental characteristics may all influence macaque behaviour, which is extremely sociable with complex social hierarchies. The body language, vocalisations, and facial expressions of macaques can reveal their intents, mood, and state of arousal.

To ensure safe and cooperative interactions with macaques, it's important to establish rapport and trust. To prevent alarming or disturbing macaques, carers should approach them carefully, speak softly, and avoid making sudden movements or loud noises. Building trust and creating a good connection with handling may be aided by offering food incentives, engaging in pleasant conversations, and respecting their personal space.

Reducing Anxiety and Stress: Macaques may experience stress during handling, particularly if they are unfamiliar with the technique or feel threatened. To alleviate stress and anxiety, carers should avoid circumstances that may cause their patients to feel fearful or uncomfortable, reassure and support them, and manage their patients with care. Positive reinforcement, familiarity with routines, and progressive desensitisation can all help to reduce tension and provide a sense of security.

Using suitable restraint measures is crucial for the safety of both macaques and their carers. To avoid harm or discomfort, restraint should be strong yet mild, never intimidating. Excessive force and pressure should be avoided. Depending on the conditions and the macaque's behaviour, a variety of methods can be used, such as towel wrapping, physical restraint, or specialised gadgets.

Customised Management Strategies: Macaques should have handling strategies tailored to their own requirements, preferences, and temperament. Some macaques may be more responsive or reactive than others to handling and interaction. To guarantee a positive and stress-free experience, carers should observe and analyse each macaque's behaviour, communicate effectively with them, and alter handling procedures as appropriate.

Positive reinforcement approaches can increase cooperative behaviour and reinforce desired answers. Macaques can be persuaded to participate freely in handling activities by offering food incentives, vocal praise, or tactile reinforcement immediately following desirable behaviours. This helps to create a good relationship with handling. To encourage positive behaviour and trust, rewards must be distributed on a timely and regular basis.

Environmental Factors to Consider.

Temperature, noise level, illumination, and cage design are examples of environmental factors that influence macaque handling sessions. It is preferable to manage in a quiet, controlled environment free of distractions or disruptions that may cause stress or anxiety. Adequate lighting and acceptable temperatures are critical for the comfort and well-being of macaques and carers when being handled.

Successful and safe handling methods need efficient coordination and communication among carers. When handling, carers should synchronise motions and activities with verbal cues, hand signs, or other means of communication. They must also communicate with one another in a clear and straightforward manner. Handling sessions may be made more efficient and fluid by planning ahead of time, teaching handling protocols, and practicing them.

Carers must be prepared to respond quickly and aggressively in emergency situations, including medical issues, hostile behaviour, and escape attempts. Establishing and teaching all carers on emergency protocols that outline how to assess hazards, ask for help, and handle emergencies is a smart idea. To respond swiftly to catastrophes, communication devices, emergency equipment, and first aid supplies must be readily available.

When dealing with macaques, carers should wear appropriate personal protective equipment (PPE) to prevent accidents and disease transmission. To avoid scratches, bites, and contact with body fluids, gloves, goggles, facemasks, and eyeglasses may be required. Personal protective equipment (PPE) must be properly fitted, maintained, and updated as needed to provide optimal protection.

Preventing the Spread of Zoonotic illnesses: Humans can get zoonotic illnesses from macaques through direct contact, bites, scratches, or infected bodily fluids. To prevent the transmission of zoonotic infections when handling, carers should wear personal protection equipment (PPE), practise excellent hygiene, and follow sanitation guidelines. To limit the risk of zoonotic disease transmission, it is critical to wash your hands often, disinfect your equipment, and handle potentially contaminated things with care.

Safe and successful handling of macaques requires ongoing education, skill development, and training. Before undertaking any handling activities, carers should get extensive instruction on macaque behaviour, handling techniques, safety considerations, and emergency protocols. Maintaining proficiency and ensuring the safety of macaques and carers necessitates continual instruction, skill evaluation, and regular practice sessions.

To summarise, ensuring the health and welfare of macaques and their carers in captivity necessitates cautious handling and attention to safety protocols. Carers can help macaques have safe, enjoyable, and stress-free handling experiences by being aware of their behaviour, establishing rapport and trust, reducing stress and anxiety, employing appropriate restraint techniques, tailoring handling approaches, and engaging in effective communication and coordination. Preparing for emergencies, following safety measures, and offering continual training are critical for ensuring a safe and stimulating environment for macaques in captivity.

Chapter 9

Typical Problems and Fixes for Macaque Care

Taking care of macaques in captivity involves unique challenges, ranging from social dynamics and habitat enrichment to behavioural disorders and health concerns. In order to enhance the welfare, health, and well-being of macaques held in captivity, we will investigate some of the common issues with macaque care and suggest feasible solutions.

Macaques may be challenging to care for owing to their aggressive, stereotyped, and social behaviours. Resource rivalry, territorial conflicts, arguments about social status, or reproductive behaviour can all lead to aggression among macaques. Pacing, rocking, and self-harming behaviours are examples of stereotypical acts that might be triggered by stress, boredom, or irritation.

Resolution:

Determine the fundamental causes: To determine the roots of aggressiveness or stereotyped behaviours in macaques, carers should pay close attention to the animals' behaviour. Understanding the underlying reason can help with the development of tailored interventions.

Environmental enrichment: Provide puzzle feeders, climbing frames, and socialising opportunities as examples of how to provide a stimulating environment for the mind and body. Boredom and tension can be decreased by enrichment activities, lowering the likelihood of stereotyped behaviour.

Social management entails providing adequate space, resources, and chances for socialisation in order to assist

60

govern social dynamics within macaque groups. To minimise disagreements and maintain a healthy social order, introduce new members gradually and monitor interactions closely.

Health risks for macaques include parasite infestations, viral infections, dental difficulties, and metabolic abnormalities. Stress, insufficient shelter, and poor diet may all impair the immune system, making people more susceptible to sickness. To maintain macaques' health and well-being, health problems must be detected early and treated promptly.

Resolution:

Schedule frequent veterinarian visits to monitor your macaque's health, detect early signs of sickness, and provide preventative treatment like as immunisations and parasite prevention.

To achieve their dietary requirements, macaques must consume a well-balanced diet rich in fruits, vegetables, grains, and protein. Consult a nutritionist or veterinarian to develop food regimens that are tailored to each macaque's specific requirements.

Environmental management: To limit the risk of infectious illnesses and respiratory issues, keep living circumstances clean and sanitary, with enough ventilation and appropriate temperature and humidity levels. Enclosures should be cleaned, disinfected, and provided with access to clean water on a regular basis.

Enriching the habitat can promote natural behaviours, prevent boredom, and increase macaques' overall well-being. However, it might be challenging to design exciting situations that meet the diverse demands of macaques.

Resolution:

Provide a variety of enrichment possibilities, such as climbing frames, perplexing feeders, foraging opportunities, strange things, and chances to socialise. Rotate enrichment items on a regular basis to keep them interesting and avoid boredom.

Enrichment activities should be tailored to the preferences and behaviours of certain species, such as macaques. When selecting enrichment alternatives, consider individual temperament, age, gender, and social standing.

Environmental complexity: Create dynamic, multidimensional places that promote social interaction, problem solving, and discovery. To imitate the complexity of macaque natural settings, include actual components such as water features, vegetation, and rocks.

Macaques have complex social structures, including interactions, affiliative connections, and dominance hierarchies. Controlling social dynamics in macaque groups can be challenging, especially when new members are introduced or conflicts arise.

Resolution:

Gradual introductions: Allow new macaques to adjust to group dynamics and build social ties by gradually introducing them into existing groups. Keep an eye on introductions and intervene if there are any disputes.

Opportunities for socialisation: Allow macaques to socialise, groom, play, and collaborate. Socialisation fosters a sense of belonging to the group, reduces stress, and promotes beneficial connections.

Behavioural management: Keep an eye on macaque behaviour and take proactive steps to prevent clashes or hostility. Reduce tension and competitiveness by implementing social management tactics such as providing ample space, resources, and socialising opportunities.

Reproductive management is vital in caring for macaques, particularly in breeding colonies or institutions that require contraception to prevent overcrowding. Nonetheless, managing sexual behaviour and adhering to contraceptive measures may be tough and confusing.

Resolution:

Options for contraception: Consult a veterinary professional to determine the optimum means of contraception for macaques, taking into account their age, gender, health, and fertility status. Surgical sterilisation, hormonal contraception, and behavioural management techniques are all viable possibilities.

Observing reproductive behaviour: Keep an eye out for signs of estrus, mating behaviour, or pregnancy in macaques. Adopt contraception methods as needed to regulate population dynamics and prevent undesired pregnancies.

Breeding management: If you want to breed, carefully choose breeding couples based on temperament, genetic variety, and general health. Follow breeding management practices to increase reproduction success while also ensuring the well-being of parents and offspring.

Training macaques for cooperative care and handling is essential for efficient medical treatments, behavioural control, and veterinary exams. However, educating macaques may be time-consuming and requires certain talents, effort, and patience.

Resolution:

Positive reinforcement training is used to teach macaques cooperative care behaviours such as remaining still, displaying body parts, and happily participating in medical operations. To build good associations with handling, reward desired behaviours with food, verbal praise, or tactile reinforcement.

Desensitisation strategies should be used to progressively introduce macaques to medical procedures and equipment. When rewarding calm, relaxed behaviour, begin with low-intensity stimuli and gradually raise the amount of stimulus over time.

Customised training programmes: Create training regimens for each macaque based on their own needs, preferences, and abilities. When developing training procedures to maximise achievement and reduce stress, consider elements such as temperament, past experiences, and learning styles.

To summarise, taking appropriate care of macaques in captivity presents a variety of obstacles that need careful planning and proactive management strategies. Carers may improve the health, welfare, and well-being of macaques in captivity by addressing common difficulties such as behavioural disorders, health concerns, environmental enrichment, social dynamics, reproductive control, and training and handling practices. Putting into practice feasible solutions tailored to each macaque's specific requirements and characteristics can help to provide a safe, exciting, and serene environment for these remarkable monkeys.

Chapter 10

Having a Happy and Meaningful Bond with Your Macaque Pet

Although caring for a macaque companion may be a rewarding and enlightening experience, there are some unique challenges and responsibilities associated. To form a strong and rewarding relationship with your macaque, you must devote time, understanding, and devotion to meeting his or her physical, social, and emotional requirements. In this in-depth research, we will look at the key concepts, strategies, and criteria for creating a calm and satisfying connection with your macaque companion.

Understanding your macaque companion's behaviour, social structure, and communication signs is essential for developing a deep link with them. Macaques are extremely sociable creatures with complex communication networks, affiliative ties, and social hierarchies. You may learn a lot about your macaque's wants, desires, and feelings by observing their body language, vocalisations, and social interactions.

sociable structure: Macaques are sociable creatures that live in complex communities characterised by social relationships, grooming alliances, and dominance hierarchy. Understanding your macaque's social structure and how they interact with other members of the group may help you build rapport and trust with them.

Macaques interact with humans and with one another using a variety of vocalisations, facial gestures, and body postures. Understanding your macaque's objectives, emotions, and degree of arousal by learning to interpret communication signs can allow you to communicate with them more successfully and mutually comprehend.

Establishing rapport and trust with your macaque partner is essential for a strong and fulfilling friendship. To gain your macaque's confidence, you must engage in regular, positive encounters, communicate openly, and understand its individual wants and preferences.

Respect personal space: Do not force interactions or impose yourself on your macaque, and be aware of their boundaries and personal space. Allow your macaque to approach you when they are ready and comfortable, and allow them do it on their own terms.

Using positive reinforcement strategies, you may reward desired behaviours while also strengthening collaboration and trust. Giving them food incentives, vocal praise, or tactile reinforcement will help them create good connections with your presence and interactions.

Maintaining consistency and predictability in your interactions and routines with your macaque companion is essential. A safe, secure environment and a consistent daily programme can help your macaque experience less fear and develop confidence and trust.

Macaques require both mental and physical engagement for optimal health and behaviour. A variety of toys, social connections, and hobbies may help your kid avoid boredom, reduce stress, and enhance overall mental and physical health.

Environmental enrichment: Provide opportunities for your macaque companion to explore, climb, forage, and socialise in a bright and engaging surroundings. Use realistic elements such as branches, pebbles, and hiding spots to mimic their natural environment and encourage their natural instincts.

Give your macaque a variety of interactive toys, puzzle feeders, and enrichment items to challenge his or her problem-solving ability and provide cerebral stimulation. To keep things interesting and minimise repetition, replace toys and enrichment materials on a regular basis.

Socialisation possibilities: Ensure that your macaque partner gets regular opportunity to socialise with other macaques, friendly animal friends, or trustworthy people. Social engagement helps to reduce stress, provide a sense of security and belonging, and promote emotional well-being.

Handle with respect and care:

When handling and caring for your macaque friend, always be kind, respectful, and considerate of their needs and preferences. To keep your macaque healthy and happy, you must handle them carefully, provide routine veterinarian treatment, and keep a watchful eye on them.

Gentle handling: Avoid sudden movements or harsh handling that may startle or upset your macaque friend. Instead, show them tenderness and respect. Use positive reinforcement tactics to encourage cooperative behaviour and create good connections with handling and caring.

Schedule preventative care and routine veterinarian checks for your macaque friend to monitor their health, detect early signs of sickness, and administer immunisations and parasite control medicines. To ensure your macaque's health and well-being, follow your veterinarian's food, grooming, and medicinal guidelines.

Observational monitoring: Keep an eye out for any changes or signs of concern in your macaque companion's behaviour, appetite, or overall health. Early detection of behavioural changes or health difficulties can aid in preventing or treating problems before they worsen.

Developing a solid relationship with your macaque partner requires effective communication and mutual understanding. Here are some activities to help. Communication is two-way street. Spending quality time with your dog and engaging in bonding activities might help to deepen your relationship.

To comfort your macaque companion and provide a sense of trust and security, speak to them in a soothing, quiet tone. Use clear verbal signals and orders to communicate expectations and encourage desired behaviour.

Nonverbal communication: Use nonverbal indicators like as body language, gestures, and facial expressions to communicate your emotions, intentions, and moods with your macaque partner. To maintain mutual understanding and trust, observe your macaque's behaviours and responses and adjust your communication method accordingly.

Activities that promote bonding: Take your macaque companion on grooming sessions, engaging play dates, training sessions, or outdoor trips, among other things. Spending quality time together strengthens your relationship and fosters a sense of camaraderie and affection.

Personal Preferences and Needs: Each companion macaque has unique personality, likes, and needs. Building a trusting and meaningful connection with your animal necessitates embracing and honouring its individuality, as well as mutual understanding.

Customised care and enrichment: Tailor the activities you give for your children to their specific needs, interests, and abilities. When selecting toys, activities, and socialisation chances, keep age, gender, temperament, and previous experiences in mind.

Flexibility and agility are essential while caring for your macaque friend. You should be prepared to adjust your daily routine and activities to meet their changing demands and preferences. Pay attention to your macaque's cues and actions, and respond to their calls and motions.

Recognise that your macaque partner has feelings, needs, and experiences that are unique to them, and treat them with care, compassion, and understanding. In times of stress, worry, or uncertainty, be understanding and supportive while also providing comfort and confidence.

To summarise, having a happy and fulfilling relationship with your macaque buddy requires patience, empathy, and a commitment to meeting their social, emotional, and physical needs. You may form a deep and meaningful relationship with your macaque partner that improves both of your lives by learning about macaque behaviour, creating rapport and trust with them, providing suitable stimulation and care, and respecting their individuality. Always remember to show your macaque friend love, respect, and thanks for the amazing relationship you have.

Chapter 11

Frequently Asked Questions (FAQs) concerning Owning Pet Macaques

Can humans keep macaques as pets?

Macaques are not advised as pets due to their complex needs, unusual care requirements, and explosive temperament. They are also prohibited in many locations. Macaques are wild animals with strong territorial and social tendencies that can be difficult to connect with in a domestic setting.

What legal consequences come with keeping macaques as pets?

The regulations limiting macaque ownership and possession vary by location and can range from strict limitations to full prohibitions. Macaques are protected animals in many regions, and keeping them as pets without the proper licences or permissions is illegal. Breaking these restrictions might result in significant penalties, the animal being taken away, and legal consequences.

What challenges occur from keeping macaques as pets?

The demands of macaques' social and behavioural development, their specific nutritional requirements, their proclivity for aggressiveness, and their susceptibility to zoonotic infections make maintaining them as pets challenging. Macaques are exceptionally clever, active creatures who require a lot of space, social connection, and environmental enrichment—all of which can be difficult to offer in a household setting—to thrive.

Do macaques offer any health hazards to those who keep them as pets?

Indeed, keeping macaques as pets poses a variety of health dangers, including the transmission of zoonotic infections such as hepatitis, TB, and the herpes B virus. In addition, macaques may carry germs, viruses, and parasites that humans might catch by biting, scratching, or direct contact.

How much space is required for macaques as pets?

Macaques have considerable space requirements to meet their behavioural and physical demands. Large outdoor cages or specialised primate facilities that allow for climbing, foraging, and social contact would be perfect environments for them. In a domestic setting, it is nearly hard to provide a macaque with the space and stimulation it requires to thrive.

What foods are appropriate for macaques as pets?

A varied and well-balanced meal that resembles macaques' natural wild eating patterns is required. This includes various fruits, vegetables, cereals, seeds, nuts, and protein sources. It can be difficult to provide a nutritionally adequate food for a macaque, and this may need specialised expertise and access to veterinary care.

Are macaques violent when kept as pets?

Indeed, macaques are capable of aggressive behaviour, particularly when they feel stress, danger, or being cornered. In the house, macaques may exhibit dominance displays, protective behaviours, or territorial violence, putting their owners and other inhabitants' safety at risk.

Are macaques docile enough to be pets?

Macaques are intelligent animals who can learn a variety of abilities through positive reinforcement training; yet, training them as pets can be challenging owing to their complicated social behaviours and untamed impulses. Furthermore, most pet owners lack the specialised expertise, experience, and money required to educate a macaque.

How should I respond if I see a macaque in the wild?

It's critical to preserve your distance from macaques in the wild and avoid going too near or attempting to pet them. Macaques, like wild creatures, may perceive humans as a threat, especially if they are surrounded or irritated. Allow them room and maintain a safe distance to limit the possibility of animosity or injury.

How can I contribute to the conservation of macaques?

Donations, volunteer labour, and lobbying can all assist to fund macaque conservation initiatives, therefore saving natural populations and ecosystems. Contributing to organisations that support monkey conservation, habitat preservation, and community engagement can help secure the long-term survival and well-being of macaques in the wild.

Printed in Great Britain
by Amazon